# ELIZABETH I

QUEEN OF TUDOR ENGLAND

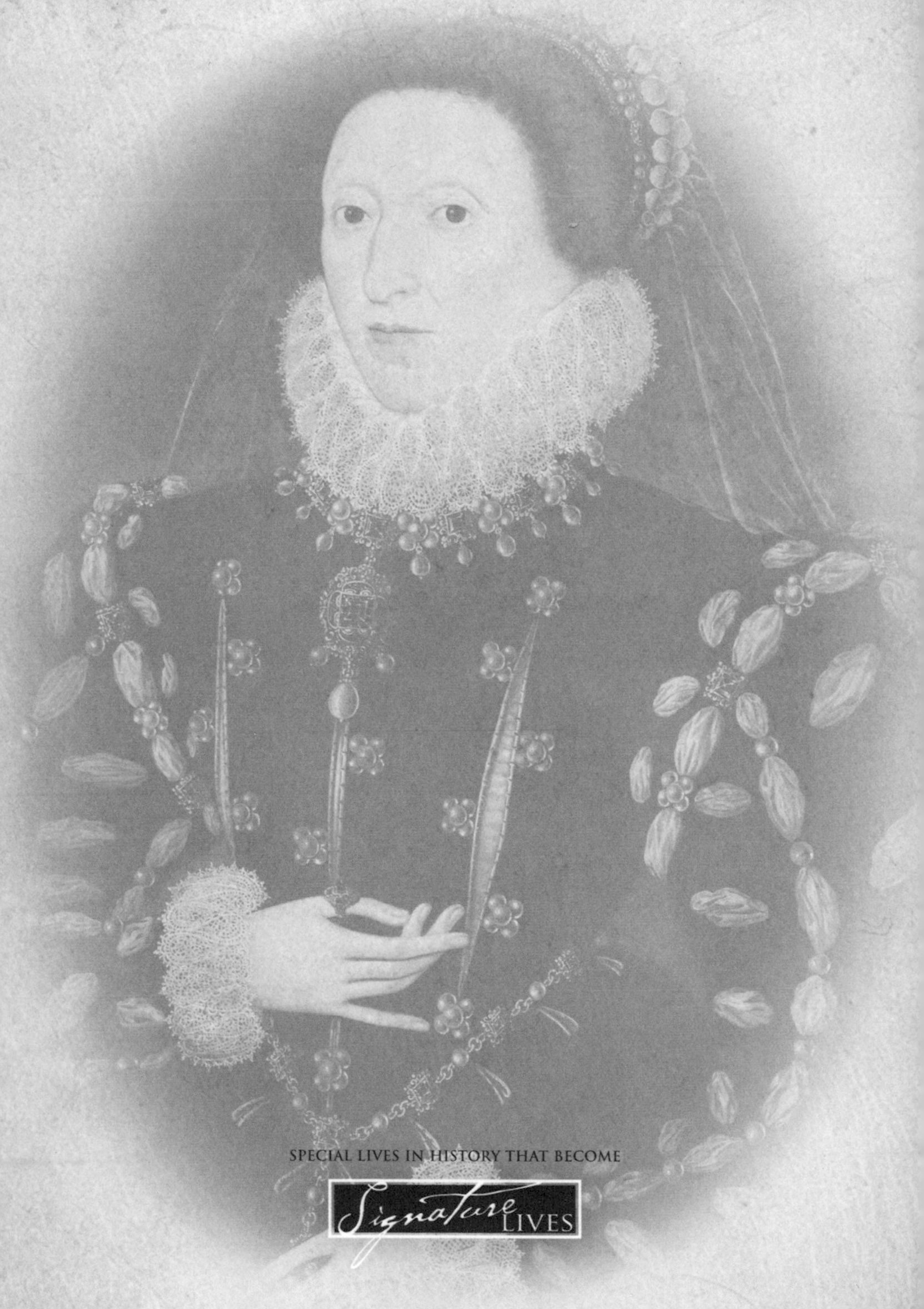
SPECIAL LIVES IN HISTORY THAT BECOME
Signature LIVES

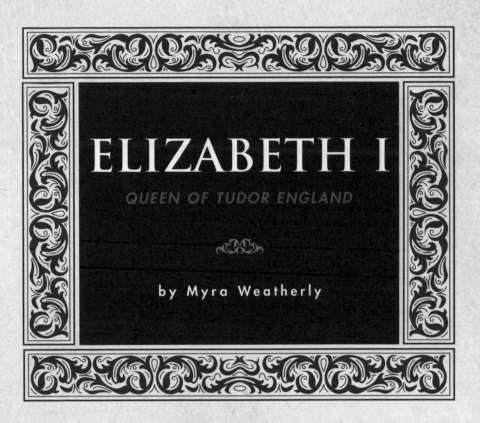

# ELIZABETH I

## QUEEN OF TUDOR ENGLAND

by Myra Weatherly

Content Adviser: Professor Arthur J. Slavin,
Justus Bier Distinguished Professor Emeritus,
University of Louisville

Reading Adviser: Rosemary G. Palmer, Ph.D.,
Department of Literacy, College of Education,
Boise State University

COMPASS POINT BOOKS  MINNEAPOLIS, MINNESOTA

Compass Point Books
3109 West 50th Street, #115
Minneapolis, MN 55410

Visit Compass Point Books on the Internet at *www.compasspointbooks.com*
or e-mail your request to *custserv@compasspointbooks.com*.


Editor: Sue Vander Hook
Lead Designer: Jaime Martens
Page Production: Heather Griffin
Photo Researcher: Svetlana Zhurkin
Cartographer: XNR Productions, Inc.
Educational Consultant: Diane Smolinski


Managing Editor: Catherine Neitge
Creative Director: Keith Griffin
Editorial Director: Carol Jones

**Library of Congress Cataloging-in-Publication Data**
Weatherly, Myra
    Elizabeth I : Queen of Tudor England / by Myra Weatherly
        v. cm—(Signature lives)
    Includes bibliographical references and index.
    ISBN-13: 978-0-7565-0988-0 (hardcover)
    ISBN-10: 0-7565-0988-2 (hardcover)
    ISBN-13: 978-0-7565-1861-5 (paperback)
    ISBN-10: 0-7565-1861-X (paperback)
I. Elizabeth I, Queen of England, 1533–1603—Juvenile literature. 2.
Great Britain—History—Elizabeth, 1558–1603—Juvenile literature. 3.
Queens—Great Britain—Biography—Juvenile literature. I. Title. II.
Series.
    DA355.W35 2005
    942.05'5'092—dc22                                    2005002790

*Signature Lives*

# RENAISSANCE ERA

The Renaissance was a cultural movement that started in Italy in the early 1300s. The word *renaissance* comes from a Latin word meaning "rebirth," and during this time, Europe experienced a rebirth of interest and achievement in the arts, science, and global exploration. People reacted against the religion-centered culture of the Middle Ages to find greater value in the human world. By the time the Renaissance came to a close, around 1600, people had come to look at their world in a brand new way.

Elizabeth I

# Table of Contents

Princess Prisoner  **9**

Lady Elizabeth  **17**

The King Is Dead  **27**

Long Live the Queen  **39**

Elizabeth Should Marry  **49**

Struggle for Peace  **57**

Entertaining Royalty  **71**

War with Spain  **79**

End of an Age  **87**


Life and Times  **96**

Life at a Glance  **102**

Additional Resources  **103**

Glossary  **105**

Source Notes  **106**

Select Bibliography  **108**

Index  **109**

Image Credits  **112**

# 1 PRINCESS PRISONER

❦

**P**alm Sunday 1554 dawned dark and dismal in London, England. Pouring rain pelted the barge on the Thames River outside the foreboding Tower of London. Onboard was a princess, drenched from the rain and terrified for her life. Twenty-one-year-old Elizabeth was on her way to prison. It didn't matter that she was heir to the throne of England. It didn't matter that her sister Mary was the queen. In fact, it was Queen Mary who had banished her to the Tower. The charge against her was conspiracy— plotting with Sir Thomas Wyatt to kill the queen. Elizabeth denied the charges, but Mary ignored her protests of innocence.

Elizabeth trembled in fear. Would she ever be released from the Tower? The barge quietly made its

*The Tower of London in the 16th century; prisoners entered through Traitor's Gate (bottom center).*

way through the entrance, fittingly called Traitor's Gate. Inside, the water lapped the stone steps. Elizabeth refused to leave the boat, complaining that her shoes would get wet. But she had no choice, the queen's courtier informed her.

Finally, Elizabeth stepped out of the barge and splashed onto the wet stairs. Above her, chained prisoners shivered in the cold rain, and heads of traitors rotted on poles. Heavily armed guards waited to receive her. Elizabeth declared:

> *Here landeth as true a subject, being prisoner, as ever landed at these stairs. Before Thee, O God, do I speak it, having no other friend but Thee alone.*

She sloshed to the top step and sank down on the cold, wet flagstones. "You were best come out of the rain, madam, for here you sit unwholesomely," pleaded the Tower lieutenant.

"It is better sitting here than in a worse place, for God knoweth, I know not, whither you will bring me," replied Elizabeth. Hearing this, her manservant began to sob uncontrollably. Elizabeth scolded him harshly. She did not need anyone weeping for her; she was innocent. She would bravely meet her fate.

Before her loomed a maze of buildings and courtyards that served as home to English royalty and a fort for military protection. Among the

buildings rose lofty towers—the White Tower, the Bloody Tower, the Bell Tower, and others. Elizabeth's own mother, Anne Boleyn, had been a prisoner in one of these towers. This day, one of them would become Elizabeth's prison as well.

*The stairs inside Traitor's Gate at the Tower of London led to Princess Elizabeth's prison.*

The guards escorted the young princess to the Bell Tower. She swiftly went to her chambers, where she lived for the next two months. Prison life for

Elizabeth was different than that of the common prisoner. She had four rooms and at least a dozen attendants who took care of her needs. Trusted servants delivered food to her daily after inspecting it for any sign of poison. They were careful to make sure someone did not try to get rid of the heir to the throne of England.

After about a month, Elizabeth was allowed to walk outside in the walled Tower Garden. But in spite of her special treatment, she worried daily that she might be executed. She often was overwhelmed by the memories of friends and family members who had lost their heads in the nearby courtyard known as Tower Green. Her mother had been executed there when Elizabeth was only 3 years old.

Two months passed, and Queen Mary took the advice of her royal council—Elizabeth should no longer remain a prisoner at the Tower. But they would not just let her go. She must be put some-where under house arrest, where she could be guarded and not allowed to leave. The council chose Woodstock, a decrepit old royal hunting lodge about 50 miles (80 kilometers) away. On May 19, 1554, a force of 100 royal guards escorted Elizabeth there, where she would live for almost a year.

Life in the rest of England was complicated and dangerous. Religious differences were causing bloodshed. Queen Mary didn't like it that her father,

*Elizabeth went hunting while she was under house arrest at Woodstock, England.*

King Henry VIII, had established the Protestant Church of England. She wanted to change England back to the way it used to be—a Roman Catholic country ruled by the pope. The conflict grew, and Protestants started losing their lives for speaking out against the Roman Catholic Church. Queen Mary was responsible for their deaths. She didn't want anyone upsetting her plan, and she got rid of anyone who tried.

*John Rogers (1500-1555) was burned for speaking out against the Roman Catholic Church. He was the first martyr of the Marian (of Mary) persecution.*

John Rogers, a Protestant minister of the Church of St. Sepulcher, was her first victim. He dared to preach against the "pestilent Popery, idolatry and superstition" of the Roman Catholic Church. After being tried for heresy and imprisoned, he was burned at the stake on February 4, 1555. Thomas Cranmer, archbishop of Canterbury, was burned that year, too. Hundreds more died for their religious beliefs under the reign of this queen who came to be known as Bloody Mary.

Meanwhile, Elizabeth lived quietly under house

arrest at Woodstock. Little did she know that in less than four years, she would become queen of England. She did not know then that one day she would resolve these religious conflicts and bring peace and prosperity to England. Her reign would be called the Golden Age of England. Some would call it the Elizabethan Age. Many would one day fondly call England's highly respected leader Good Queen Bess.

For now, Elizabeth pondered the charges Mary had brought against her. On a windowpane, she scratched these words with a diamond:

> *Much suspected, by me*
> *Nothing proved can be*
> *Quoth Elizabeth, prisoner*

It would not be long before Elizabeth would be released from her quiet prison and start serving her beloved citizens of England. ✍

# 2 LADY ELIZABETH

❧❧❧

Becoming queen of England would come naturally for Elizabeth. After all, she had been raised as the king's daughter, first in line to inherit the throne. But her father, King Henry VIII of the House of Tudor, had never been happy with this prospect. Long before Elizabeth was born, he had worried about producing a male heir to the throne. The people of England had long become accustomed to being ruled by a king. When a king died, his son immediately took over the throne. If a king did not have a son, he might appoint a male cousin or brother-in-law to succeed him.

For hundreds of years, the people of England had welcomed princes into the world. It was an important event when a future king of England was

*Elizabeth's mother was Anne Boleyn (1507-1536); her father was King Henry VIII of England (1491-1547).*

born. The excitement over Henry's children was no different. Every time Henry's first wife, Catharine of Aragon, gave birth, the people eagerly waited to hear if it was a son. But in the end, only one of their children lived—a daughter named Mary.

Angry that he had no son, Henry figured out a way to divorce Catharine. Divorce was against the rules of the Roman Catholic Church, the official religion of England. But Henry got around that rule. He established his own church and changed the official religion. The Church of England was not Roman Catholic, and it wasn't ruled by the pope. Henry's church was Protestant, and the king was in

*King Henry VIII and his daughter, Mary; a court jester stands in the background.*

charge. Henry then divorced Catharine and married Anne Boleyn. He was sure she would give him a son.

In September 1533, Anne was ready to deliver her first baby, and she was certain it was a boy. Even the king's best astrologers were sure there would now be a male heir to the throne of England. The people of England waited to hear news of the royal birth that was about to take place at Greenwich Palace in London. King Henry had ordered an elaborate celebration to honor the birth of his first son.

On September 7, the queen gave birth to the royal child. But it was not a son. She delivered a baby girl. Henry immediately canceled the celebration. There would be no pageant or jousting for the birth of a daughter. The king now had two daughters, 17-year-old Mary and this baby girl, and he was angry. Two wives had failed to give him a son. Anne would later pay for her failure.

In spite of his displeasure, King Henry went ahead with the christening three days later, as scheduled. The political elite of London assembled for the ceremony in the richly adorned Friar's Chapel at Greenwich. The bishop of London anointed the infant with oil and christened her "the right high, right noble, and right excellent Princess Elizabeth, princess of England." Hundreds of guards carrying lighted torches then escorted the new little princess back to the palace.

_In 16th-century England, babies received a first name at their christening. There was no middle name, and the last name was inherited from the child's father. Since first names got confusing, people sometimes had bynames that described them or told where they were from— William Short, Edward Berkshire. Dukes and earls were referred to by the territory they governed—the Duke of Essex was called Essex. Kings and queens used their first names with a Roman numeral to designate which monarch they were. Their last name was part of their title. It was called their "house"—the House of Tudor or the House of Stuart. Elizabeth's father, Henry Tudor, was King Henry VIII of the House of Tudor._

Although Elizabeth's birth may have been the greatest disappointment of her father's life, he still proclaimed her heir to the throne. At that moment, Mary lost her position as the future queen of England to a newborn baby. But Mary refused to accept this unless she was "compelled by sheer force."

Baby Elizabeth spent her first three months in the royal nursery at Greenwich Palace. Many servants tended to her needs. One fed her, one changed her, another rocked her cradle, and yet another did her laundry. But then, at the age of 3 months, and according to royal custom, Elizabeth was separated from her parents and removed from the palace. Attendants carried her to a lavishly decorated litter and took her on a procession through the streets of London. Her escort, her great uncle and Duke of Norfolk, would take her to her new home.

Elizabeth arrived at Hatfield, a palace north of London that her father had prepared for his royal children. There, she was placed in her satin cradle and tended to by the palace staff. Her great uncle left, but he would return. He was on his way to get Princess Mary, who would serve as a lady-in-waiting to her infant sister. The king's first daughter was now a mere servant.

Elizabeth's nurse, or main caretaker, was Lady Margaret Bryan. Every day, she managed Elizabeth's upbringing, deciding what she would wear, what she would eat, and whom she would see. Elizabeth's mother still had a small part in her daughter's upbringing. She ordered Elizabeth's elaborate

*Hatfield House, the royal palace where Elizabeth lived as a child*

clothes, as fine clothes were a symbol of high social status. But Elizabeth did not see her mother or father very often. Sometimes they would visit her at Hatfield. Other times, usually at Christmas, Elizabeth and Mary would be brought to Greenwich.

For the next three years, her parents' relationship was strained. Anne was still trying to give Henry a son. She became pregnant three more times, but none of the babies lived long enough to be born. Henry grew to detest his wife and decided that perhaps a third wife might give him a son. But first he had to get rid of Anne.

King Henry brought a variety of criminal charges against his wife. Although they could not be proved, Anne Boleyn was still convicted and sentenced. Three-year-old Elizabeth was at Hatfield on May 19, 1536, when her mother was decapitated on Tower Green at the Tower of London. The powerful king had successfully eliminated this wife who had failed to provide a male heir to the English throne. Although Elizabeth may not have known about her mother's death right away, she knew her life changed drastically that day.

Immediately, Elizabeth, Mary, and Lady Bryan left Hatfield and were taken to a different home in Hunsdon. The king had taken away Elizabeth's right to the throne, and she was no longer a princess. Elizabeth seemed to be aware of this change. In the

weeks after her mother's death, she asked her governor, "How haps it, Governor, yesterday my Lady Princess, and today but my Lady Elizabeth?"

The king and his council began to ignore Elizabeth, even neglecting to provide her with clothes that fit well. Lady Bryan wrote a letter about Elizabeth's situation to one of England's top statesmen, Thomas Cromwell. The child was outgrowing her clothes, she wrote, and there was no money to dress her properly.

At the royal court, King Henry was happy and hopeful once more. His first wife Catharine had died, and Anne had been executed. Now he could

*King Henry VIII charged his wife Anne Boleyn with false crimes and had her beheaded in 1536.*

marry again. Just 12 days after Anne's death, the king married Jane Seymour, a lady-in-waiting to the past two queens. Whenever Elizabeth visited the palace, her new stepmother was kind to her, softening some of the tension between Elizabeth and her father.

On October 12, 1537, King Henry finally got the son he had been wanting for so long. It was a proud day for the king and a jubilant time for the people of England. Three days after the birth of Edward, 4-year-old Elizabeth and 21-year-old Mary came to the king's palace to attend the christening of their half-brother. Just nine days later, the baby's mother died of an infection called childbed fever. Edward then went to live with his sisters. The palace chosen for them was the one at Hatfield.

*Edward (1537-1553), son of King Henry VIII, became heir to the throne of England.*

The royal children moved often from one country palace to another. Keeping them out of the crowded city of London reduced their chances of getting ill. It also was customary to move to another palace while one was being cleaned. Elizabeth spent most of her childhood moving about southern England, living at Hatfield House, Ashridge House, Enfield Palace, and Elsynge Place.

Prince Edward's birth changed young Elizabeth's life. Lady Bryan had to care for the new baby now, so she was no longer Elizabeth's nurse. Katherine "Kat" Champernowne became her nurse. Kat truly cared about Elizabeth and helped soften the blow of losing Lady Bryan. Elizabeth had great respect for her new nurse, and Kat was devoted to the young girl. Years later, Elizabeth told how Kat had "taken great labour and pain in bringing me up in learning and honesty."

Kat was quite well educated and became Elizabeth's governess, teaching her history, mathematics, geography, and astronomy. She educated Elizabeth in the things that royal ladies should know—needlework, dancing, and riding. By the age of 5, Elizabeth could sew. She made a lovely cambric shirt for her brother, for whom she had developed a warm affection.

Kat was with Elizabeth for many years. She watched Elizabeth grow and learn. She was with her through her teenage years and admired the mature young woman she was becoming. However, Kat did not know she was nurturing a child who would one day be queen. ♊

# 3 THE KING IS DEAD

❦

When Elizabeth was 7 years old, her father married his fourth wife, Anne of Cleves, a German princess who did not speak English. Within six months, Henry decided Anne was neither refined nor attractive enough for him, and he divorced her. Two weeks later, he married young Catherine Howard, a marriage that lasted only a few months. When Henry found out Catherine was seeing another man, he had her beheaded in February 1542. She was buried near the grave of Anne Boleyn.

The death of Catherine apparently upset young Elizabeth. She had liked this stepmother who was kind to her and seated her at the queen's table when Elizabeth visited the palace. But now, Elizabeth told a friend that she would never marry. She had

*Henry VIII and his six wives, clockwise from top: Anne of Cleves, Catherine Howard, Anne Boleyn, Catharine of Aragon, Katherine Parr, and Jane Seymour.*

*Katherine Parr
(1512-1548)
was the sixth
wife of King
Henry VIII.*

certainly seen the problems in her father's marriages.

The following year, 10-year-old Elizabeth got yet another stepmother. This one would have the greatest impact on her life. Katherine Parr was a kind woman. She was devoted to Henry's children and brought them all to live with her and the king at the royal palace. The children were given fine clothes and an excellent education. Katherine even arranged for the best tutors in England to come to the palace to teach the children. Greek and Latin scholars such as William Grindal and Roger Ascham taught Elizabeth philosophy, history, speech, French, Spanish, and Italian. She also studied theology. It was important to know about religion, since political and religious leaders made decisions for the country. Her tutors were Protestants, which was good for Elizabeth and Edward, who were raised to follow the Protestant faith.

Elizabeth learned quickly and thrived on intellectual challenges. Music and needlework rounded out her education. At a time when learning was not a priority for women, Katherine Parr insisted that Elizabeth receive the best education possible.

Elizabeth enjoyed her life at the palace for three years. But in the early hours of January 28, 1547, her father died. The age-old practice of heralds immediately proclaiming a royal death did not occur that day. Instead, the king's death was kept secret for three days while noblemen plotted to seize power.

*This portrait of Princess Elizabeth was sent as a gift to Elizabeth's half-brother, King Edward VI.*

However, before Henry died, he had named 16 guardians to take care of his son Edward. One of them was Edward Seymour, the boy's uncle. Seymour convinced Parliament to also name him Edward's regent, which gave him power to control the government until the boy king came of age. Now in control, Seymour took 9-year-old Edward and 13-year-old Elizabeth to the palace at Enfield. With brother and sister together, he told them of their father's death. Edward was now king of England.

One month after Edward's coronation, Elizabeth was taken from the king's palace. She went to live in a red brick palace overlooking the Thames River in Chelsea. She didn't go alone. Accompanying her were her governess Kat, her tutor William Grindal, and her stepmother Katherine Parr. Four months later, someone else came to live there—the handsome and ambitious Thomas Seymour. He was Katherine's new husband and the brother of Henry's third wife, Jane.

Life at Chelsea was not always pleasant for Elizabeth or her brother. Seymour often acted inappropriately with Elizabeth. He wasn't kind toward Edward and once tried to seize him at gunpoint. For this, Seymour eventually was found guilty of treason and executed. But after Elizabeth lived for a year in the same house as Seymour, Katherine sent her to Hatfield for her own protection. There

*Thomas Seymour (1508-1549), younger brother of Jane Seymour, who was the third wife of King Henry VIII*

she continued her studies and occasionally wrote letters to her brother.

For six years, Edward served as king of England, although others made the decisions. But in 1553, Edward became very ill. While he lay on his sick bed, he proclaimed that he did not want his sisters to be heirs to the throne. Instead, he named his cousin Lady Jane Grey as heir.

On July 6, 1553, young King Edward VI died, and 15-year-old Lady Jane Grey became the queen of England. Mary was furious and claimed she was the rightful heir to the throne. Jane had served as queen only nine days when Mary raised up an army of powerful supporters. She took over the throne of England without a fight. The next year, Queen Mary had Jane beheaded.

Amid all this turmoil, Elizabeth lived quietly at Hatfield. Although she was not happy that Mary was queen, Elizabeth calmly declared her loyalty to her sister. She wrote her a letter of congratulations and departed for London to attend Mary's coronation ceremony. Elizabeth's entrance into the city on July 29, 1553, did not go unnoticed. Nineteen-year-old Elizabeth had a military escort of 2,000 horsemen wearing green and white uniforms, the official colors of the House of

> *The Protestant faith began with the Reformation, a religious movement that started in the 1500s. A German priest named Martin Luther began challenging the doctrines of the Roman Catholic Church and caused great turmoil. He taught that the Bible was the only authority in the church. He also taught that people are made righteous in the eyes of God only through faith in Christ, not by works. In 1517, Luther nailed a list of his beliefs, the Ninety-Five Theses, to the door of the Wittenberg Castle Church in Wittenberg, Germany. Thus began the Protestant Reformation.*

Tudor. When 37-year-old Mary arrived, she ordered Elizabeth's procession to march through London next to hers. The crowds cheered for Elizabeth as much as for the new queen.

. During the first part of Mary's reign, the two sisters were on friendly terms. But then differences arose—mainly religious. Mary feared that Elizabeth might take over the throne. She hated Elizabeth because she was Protestant. Mary was determined to reverse what her father had done and make England a Roman Catholic nation once again. Eventually, Mary forced Elizabeth to renounce her Protestant beliefs or die. Outwardly, Elizabeth

*Queen Mary and Princess Elizabeth entered London together in 1553.*

claimed to be Catholic. But inwardly, she still clung to her Protestant beliefs.

Elizabeth stayed at Hatfield, away from her sister and the conflicts that were pushing them further apart. But she couldn't avoid the plots and scandals. When Sir Thomas Wyatt led a rebellion against Mary in 1554, he hinted that Elizabeth was part of it. Mary immediately sent for Elizabeth to come to London for questioning. A frightened Elizabeth entered London with the curtains of her litter closed. Even so, she could see the heads and corpses of Wyatt and his followers scattered throughout the city. The gallows where they died were visible, and heads teetered on tops of poles.

Mary's royal council questioned Elizabeth harshly, but she remained strong and denied any involvement in Wyatt's rebellion. Although there was no proof of guilt, two councilors demanded that she be sent to the Tower of London. Elizabeth was horrified. Her mother had been beheaded there, and so had her stepmother Catherine Howard. Just six weeks earlier, Lady Jane Grey had been executed there as well. Elizabeth wrote a desperate letter to her sister, begging for mercy. But Mary angrily refused to read it.

On that rainy Palm Sunday morning in 1554, the citizens of London were in church. Mary's royal councilors secretly loaded Elizabeth and eight of her attendants onto the royal barge, and they made their way up the Thames River to the Tower of London. Silently floating through Traitor's Gate, the barge stopped at the wet stairs that led to the Tower. Elizabeth embarked, proclaiming:

> *Oh Lord, I never thought to have come in here as a prisoner, and I pray you all bear me witness that I come in as no traitor but as true a woman to the Queen's Majesty as any as is now living.*

*Princess Elizabeth in prison at the Tower of London*

Elizabeth was now a prisoner. She walked bravely to the Bell Tower and entered the darkest period of her life. Although she was released to Woodstock for a time and then to Hatfield, she lived in fear of Mary and stayed out of the affairs of England.

Religious tensions increased under Mary's reign. The queen was working hard to restore England to a Catholic nation. She even married King Philip II

*Mary I was queen of England from 1553-1558. She was nicknamed Bloody Mary for killing hundreds of Protestants.*

of Spain, a Catholic. His father was the holy Roman emperor, who agreed to help return England to the Catholic religion. Mary took action to resolve the Protestant problem by executing hundreds of outspoken Protestants. After all, she reasoned, they were heretics who dared to disagree with the Roman Catholic Church.

The people of England began to dislike Bloody Mary. They didn't like her religious endeavors, and they didn't like her husband. To make matters worse, the country was suffering from poverty and famine. The people also worried about the future of England. Mary had not produced an heir to the throne, and now she probably was too old to do so. The citizens' hopes were raised twice when Mary claimed to be pregnant.

But as it turned out, she had made up those claims. There were no pregnancies, and she became a laughingstock. Eventually, Philip II found no reason to stay in England. He disliked the country, and his wife could not produce a Spanish heir to the English throne. In addition, Mary was seriously ill. He returned to Spain after reminding Mary to treat Elizabeth well. ❧

# 4 LONG LIVE THE QUEEN

*Chapter*

⌒⌒⌒

Queen Mary of the House of Tudor died of cancer on November 17, 1558. Bells rang out and parties erupted in the streets of London as word spread of the 42-year-old queen's death. Several royal councilors raced to Hatfield with the news. There, under an oak tree, reading a Greek Bible, they found Elizabeth. As the men approached her, Elizabeth stood up. The councilors immediately knelt before her and saluted her as queen of England. Elizabeth fell to her knees and uttered in Latin, "*A Domino factum est ilud et est mirabile in oculis nostris*" ("This is the doing of the Lord, and it is marvelous in our eyes").

Elizabeth was now queen of England. She inherited one of the most troubled thrones in Europe. It

*Queen Elizabeth I in her coronation robe*

had been plagued by religious unrest, drought, high prices, poverty, overcrowding in London, and poor relations with foreign countries. One observer wrote:

*I never saw England weaker in strength, men, and riches. ... Here was nothing but fining, beheading, hanging, quartering, and burning; taxing, levying, pulling down of bulwarks at home, and beggaring and losing our strongholds abroad.*

*During the reign of Queen Mary (1553–1558), drought plagued England. Lack of rain led to poor crops, which led to high prices for food and goods. Many people suffered financially and became very poor. Most of them flocked to London to look for jobs and find a place to live in the lower-rent districts. As a result, London became very overcrowded. This was the dismal condition of England when Elizabeth became queen in 1558.*

In addition, other people were trying to claim the English throne. Mary, Queen of Scots, Elizabeth's cousin, was one of them. The two sisters of Lady Jane Grey, who had briefly been queen, wanted to take over. Men from all over Europe now wanted to marry Elizabeth, just to have a son who could one day claim England for their country. But practical, confident Elizabeth remained calm. She held tightly to her throne, and ignored her enemies and her suitors. She began working to make England strong.

The first thing she did was form a loyal government. While still at Hatfield, she appointed her own royal council. She chose an old friend, William Cecil, as secretary of state. Robert Dudley was appointed master of the horse, who took care of the royal stables. Elizabeth even gave her longtime governess Kat a position in the royal court. She also chose a motto: *Semper Eadem* ("Always the Same"). This was very befitting a queen who had been stable throughout all her hardships.

*Robert Dudley (1532-1588) was the first earl of Leicester, England.*

With the heads of government chosen, it was now time for Elizabeth to leave Hatfield and go to London. On November 28, 1558, Queen Elizabeth, wearing a royal purple velvet dress, rode in triumph through the crowded streets of London. More than 1,000 gentlemen and ladies on horseback accompanied her. Her guards rode on each side of her, and Dudley followed behind. The people of England sang and cheered. Children gave speeches. Elizabeth's "every motion seemed a well-guided action; her eye was set upon one, her ear listened to another ... her spirit seemed to be everywhere."

Elizabeth's destination that day must have brought a flood of memories. She was on her way to the Tower of London, not as a prisoner this time, but as royalty. When she neared the Tower, her comment to Dudley was fitting:

> *Some have fallen from being Princes of this land to be prisoners in this place; I am raised from being prisoner in this place to be Prince of this land. That dejection was a work of God's justice; this advancement is a work of His mercy.*

Elizabeth stayed at the Tower for the next 10 days, making important decisions for her country. The most urgent need was to resolve the religious conflict. Although Elizabeth was a devout Protestant, she thought English citizens should be able to believe as they pleased in private. But she did require that they attend the Protestant Church of England. She wanted her people to remain loyal and obedient to her. Most of them did just that. They found it easy to follow a queen who was fair, just, and committed to her subjects.

Elizabeth and her court spent Christmas at the Whitehall Palace. In January, it was time for the queen's coronation. On January 14, 1559, Elizabeth

again returned to the Tower, where she prepared for her important day. When it came time for her to leave, Elizabeth prayed aloud:

*The Tower of London is one of the largest castles in England.*

> *O Almighty and Everlasting God, I give Thee most hearty thanks. ... Thou hast dealt as mercifully with me as Thou didst with Daniel, whom Thou delivered ... from the raging lions.*

The bystanders clapped as the lions in the Tower menagerie began to roar.

The festivities began with an elaborate procession. Elizabeth sat in her litter covered in gold brocade material. Royal servants picked up the litter by its poles and started the march through the crowded city. With the cheers of spectators ringing in her ears, Elizabeth made her way through freshly graveled and decorated streets. A light snow fell, but that did not dampen the celebration. Pageants and demonstrations studded the route.

Elizabeth was delighted with the crowds, often stopping the procession to receive flowers and allow her subjects a closer look at their new leader. They saw a slender, 25-year-old woman clad in a crimson gown made of velvet and gold cloth. A fur cape kept her warm. Strands of reddish hair framed her pale oval face as she smiled down at them.

The procession finally brought Elizabeth to Westminster, where the English Parliament met and where English monarchs had been crowned since 1066. She stayed in Westminster Hall that night. The next day, January 15, she emerged, dressed in her lavishly jeweled coronation robes. Church bells rang as she walked slowly along a blue carpet and made her way to Westminster Abbey, the national church. No sooner had she passed than the crowds began tearing the carpet to pieces as souvenirs.

As she entered Westminster Abbey, choirs sang, drums played, the organ resounded, and trumpets proclaimed the presence of royalty. Elizabeth took her place on the coronation chair and was anointed Queen Elizabeth of England. The huge royal crown was placed on her head. She graciously received the sword, the ring, and the scepter, all symbols of her position as ruler. The ceremony was a religious event, but it pleased everyone. It was a strange mixture of Roman Catholic and Protestant practices, a foreshadowing of how Elizabeth planned to rule the country.

*Crowds gather outside Westminster Abbey to see Queen Elizabeth I on her coronation day.*

As Queen Elizabeth was presented to the people, music erupted, bells pealed, and the people cheered. Elizabeth and 800 guests then made their way back to Westminster Hall for a festive coronation banquet that lasted 10 hours. Elizabeth was exhausted when it was over. She canceled her activities the next day to recover from a cold she had caught. Parliament was scheduled to open January 23, but Elizabeth postponed it two days. On January 25, she came out, and the crowds again hailed her, shouting, "God save and maintain thee!"

Elizabeth then went to work. She immediately took steps to improve her country and settle its conflicts, especially the religious ones. Parliament, made up of the House of Commons and the House of Lords, passed the Act of Supremacy. The law made the queen supreme ruler of the country in all things spiritual and earthly. It also made Protestantism the official religion of England.

The Act of Uniformity followed. It restored religious worship to the way it was under King Henry VIII. *The Book of Common Prayer*, written while Edward VI was king, was re-established, with some additions. The church still had a Catholic look with its altars, crucifixes, tapestries, and candles. But Catholic activities such as pilgrimages and reciting the rosary were gone now. All services were in English, not Latin, and priests were allowed to

*Title page of Thomas Cranmer's* The Book of Common Prayer

marry. Everyone over the age of 16 had to attend the Church of England on Sundays or pay a fine.

With many of the religious problems resolved, Parliament focused on another problem—finding a husband for Elizabeth. ✍

# 5 ELIZABETH SHOULD MARRY

☙⚬❧

Marriage was an important item on Parliament's list of things to discuss. England faced the same problem when Henry was king—who would be the next heir to the throne? The queen's marriage was also the topic of conversation among the people of England, and they had good reason to talk. Protestants feared that if Elizabeth remained single, a Catholic might take over the throne after she died. Catholics were also afraid that a Catholic takeover of the throne might cause a civil war between the two religious groups.

Members of Elizabeth's royal court began gossiping about possible husbands for the queen. She was the most promising marriage prospect in Europe, and she never lacked for suitors. Her first

*Portrait of Queen Elizabeth I, known as the Sieve Portrait, shows a sieve in her left hand, which was symbolic of virginity.*

*Elizabeth I spent all of her life in and around London, England, moving from one palace to another.*

proposal came from King Philip II of Spain, who had been married to her late sister, Mary. For some time, Elizabeth made Philip believe she was interested in him. After all, she needed his political support. But she had no intention of marrying him, since he was a Catholic.

When Parliament asked Elizabeth to get married as soon as possible, she declared, "I am already bound unto an husband, which is the kingdom of England." Stretching out her hand, she displayed her coronation ring. As for children, she said, "Everyone of you, and as many as are English, are my children and kinsfolk." Although Elizabeth listened politely to the concerns of Parliament, she refused to be told what to do.

Some thought she had her eyes on Robert Dudley, her handsome master of the horse and favorite courtier. After all, they flirted with each other almost daily, and they had a lot in common. They had known each other since childhood, and they had both been prisoners in the Tower at the same time. Whenever the queen went riding or dancing, Dudley was by her side. Elizabeth found him stimulating and fun-loving. They openly displayed their affections for each other. But Dudley was a married man.

Many Englishmen detested Dudley for his arrogance and shameless ambition. The councilors,

> *While Elizabeth was a princess, men from all over wanted to marry her. Among them were Archduke Ferdinand of Austria, Prince Frederick of Denmark, and Prince Eric of Sweden. When she became queen of England, many of these men continued to court her and try to gain her favor. New suitors also tried to win her heart. Among them were Phillip II of Spain, King Charles IX of France, Archduke Charles of Austria, and Duke Henry de Valois of Anjou. Queen Elizabeth never married and came to be known as the Virgin Queen.*

most particularly William Cecil, distrusted Dudley's unique access to the queen. They blamed him for the queen's refusal to marry one of her princely suitors. The courts of Europe were abuzz with talk of the queen of England's suspected love life.

Then on September 8, 1560, Dudley's wife, Amy, died under suspicious circumstances. Her servants found her dead at the bottom of a flight of stairs, her neck broken. Of course, Dudley was the prime suspect in his wife's mysterious death. Elizabeth could not risk a scandal, and she quickly banished Dudley from her court and ordered an inquest. The verdict proclaimed that Amy's death was an accident, although few people believed it. In fact, most people assumed Dudley murdered his wife so he could marry the queen.

Cleared of the charges, Dudley returned triumphantly to Elizabeth's court amid a flow of rumors and schemes to assassinate him. Publicly, Elizabeth supported Dudley and gave him the title Earl of Leicester. But she would not marry him, and people still worried about a successor.

Two years later, in the fall of 1562, the people's worries grew even greater when Elizabeth became very ill. Her temperature soared, and a rash broke out. Her doctors diagnosed her with smallpox, a disease that could be deadly. Elizabeth drifted in and out of consciousness, and her panic-stricken council

*Lady Amy Dudley, wife of Robert Dudley, is found dead at the bottom of the stairs in her home.*

met over the unresolved matter of succession. After hours of arguing and disagreeing, the council received word that the queen was awake and able to speak.

Her councilors quickly gathered around her bed. They wanted to hear her speak the name of the person she would appoint as the next monarch of England. She spoke a name, but her councilors were astounded. The queen had just named Robert Dudley to be Lord Protector, or ruler, of England. Then Elizabeth swore solemnly that "although she loved and had always loved Lord Robert dearly, as God was her witness, nothing improper had ever passed between them." Hiding their dismay, the councilors promised her request would be granted.

However, the queen did not die from smallpox. After she recovered, Elizabeth reversed her decision. She gave Dudley another important position, and he enjoyed even greater favor in her court.

By January 1563, Parliament was trying even harder to settle the marriage question. They begged Elizabeth to marry or at least name a successor. But she still hesitated. She was afraid people might plot to kill the person she named. She knew what that was like when she had become successor to her sister Mary's throne.

Then there was the problem of Elizabeth's cousin, Mary, Queen of Scots. Since this Catholic queen was of the House of Tudor and a relative, she had a rightful claim to the English throne. If Elizabeth could get Mary to choose a Protestant husband, then her children would be Protestant, and

England would be safe.

Elizabeth came up with a surprising idea. Mary should marry Robert Dudley. The idea was so startling that the Scottish ambassador assumed the queen was teasing. But Elizabeth was, indeed, serious. She could trust Dudley, who already was very devoted and loyal to her. If Mary were married to a Protestant English nobleman, Elizabeth would have more control over what kind of person ruled England in the future.

*Mary, Queen of Scots (1542-1587) was queen of Scotland during the reign of her cousin, Queen Elizabeth I.*

Mary was quite insulted at Elizabeth's offer of her hand-me-down companion. Dudley didn't like the idea, either, and refused to be used for political purposes. He had no desire to wed his queen's rival; he believed he still had a chance to marry Elizabeth. Mary went against Elizabeth's wishes and married someone else—Henry, Lord Darnley, of the House of Stuart and a Catholic. In England, the question of an heir to the throne remained unresolved. ✍

# 6 STRUGGLE FOR PEACE

❧⟨∽⟩❧

England's Parliament continued to meddle in Elizabeth's personal life. The marriage issue still had to be resolved. But Elizabeth ignored them and those who wanted to marry her. She stood by what she had proclaimed the year she was crowned queen:

> *And to me it shall be a full satisfaction, both for the memorial of my Name, and for my Glory also, if when I shall let my last breath, it be ingraven upon my Marble Tomb, Here lieth Elizabeth, which Reigned a Virgin, and died a Virgin.*

Elizabeth turned her attention abroad. In 1562, the morning after she came down with smallpox,

*Mary, Queen of Scots, with her husband Henry, Lord Darnley, of the House of Stuart*

she had sent troops to France to help the Protestants there. Once they arrived, her advisers lost their nerve and ordered the army to hide rather than fight. Soon, English soldiers were falling ill and dying in great numbers from the bubonic plague, a disease spread by fleas. For the safety of her soldiers, Elizabeth brought them home. However, the returning soldiers brought the disease-carrying fleas back to England with them in their luggage. The disease, which came to be called the Black Death, spread rapidly. Londoners and rural Englanders died by the thousands. Elizabeth's military ventures abroad had been a costly mistake.

Meanwhile, there were scandals in Scotland. Mary, Queen of Scots, discovered that her dashing husband Henry, Lord Darnley, was a spoiled, arrogant alcoholic. She turned to her Italian secretary, David Riccio, for companionship. Her husband raged with jealousy and plotted to

*The bubonic plague started as early as the 6th century. Rodents, especially rats, carried the bacteria. Fleas ingested the rat's blood and then moved freely to humans. The flea would bite a human, releasing some of the infected rat's blood. The disease caused high fever, sore limbs, vomiting of blood, and swelling of the lymph nodes. The swelling was large and turned a blackish color, which was the reason this disease came to be called the Black Death. For three or four days, the diseased person was in terrible pain and looked dreadful, and then died. The rat also died. But the flea lived a long life.*

murder Riccio.

In March 1566, Darnley and his hired assassins dragged Riccio from Mary's supper table. In the presence of the Scottish queen, who was six months pregnant, the intruders murdered Riccio. Elizabeth was deeply concerned with these dark events. She worried about Mary and wrote letters to her. The tension seemed to ease between the two queens.

In June 1566, Mary gave birth to a son—James VI of the House of Stuart. The baby prince was christened in the Roman Catholic Church. Mary asked Elizabeth to be the godmother to the infant, and Elizabeth accepted. She sent a gift, a gold container for baptismal water.

Darnley continued to plot against his wife, who turned to James Hepburn, Earl of Bothwell, for support. On February 10, 1567, a tremendous explosion rocked a house where Darnley was recovering from an illness. He survived the blast, but the next morning, he was strangled by a group of assassins. Mary showed no grief for her husband's death. She gave Darnley's clothing to Bothwell, who was under suspicion for the murder. A frightened jury dared not offend the queen and found Bothwell not guilty.

After the trial, events took an even more dramatic turn. Bothwell kidnapped Mary and hastily divorced his wife. Then the Queen of Scots married

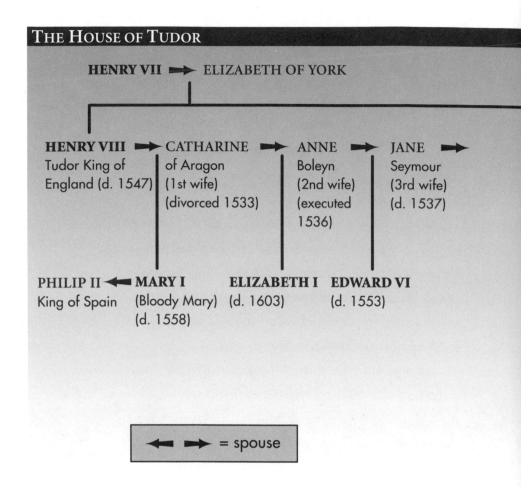

## THE HOUSE OF TUDOR

**HENRY VII** ➡ ELIZABETH OF YORK

**HENRY VIII** ➡ **CATHARINE** ➡ **ANNE** ➡ **JANE** ➡
Tudor King of    of Aragon     Boleyn     Seymour
England (d. 1547)   (1st wife)     (2nd wife)   (3rd wife)
               (divorced 1533)   (executed    (d. 1537)
                              1536)

**PHILIP II** ⬅ **MARY I**     **ELIZABETH I**   **EDWARD VI**
King of Spain   (Bloody Mary)   (d. 1603)     (d. 1553)
             (d. 1558)

⬅ ➡ = spouse

her kidnapper. Scottish leaders found the marriage shameful. Messengers hurried south to the English court with the riveting news. The events shocked all of Europe. Elizabeth was concerned about what was happening in Scotland, but she remained

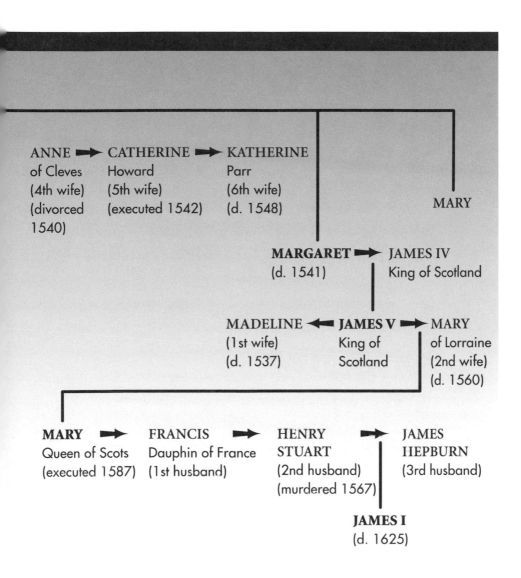

ANNE ➡ CATHERINE ➡ KATHERINE
of Cleves    Howard         Parr
(4th wife)   (5th wife)      (6th wife)
(divorced    (executed 1542) (d. 1548)
1540)

MARY

**MARGARET** ➡ JAMES IV
(d. 1541)           King of Scotland

MADELINE ◀ **JAMES V** ➡ MARY
(1st wife)    King of        of Lorraine
(d. 1537)    Scotland       (2nd wife)
                            (d. 1560)

**MARY** ➡    FRANCIS ➡        HENRY ➡    JAMES
Queen of Scots   Dauphin of France   STUART      HEPBURN
(executed 1587)  (1st husband)    (2nd husband)  (3rd husband)
                              (murdered 1567)

**JAMES I**
(d. 1625)

sympathetic to Mary.

Within a few weeks of the sensational wedding, Mary's Scottish nobles rebelled. They captured Mary, forcing her to renounce her throne in favor of her 1-year-old son, James. Bothwell escaped to

Denmark, where he eventually died in prison. In May 1568, after almost a year in captivity, Mary escaped and fled to England. She expected Elizabeth to help her regain her rights to Scotland, but Elizabeth refused.

What was Elizabeth to do with this uninvited guest? She had several options—return Mary to her Scottish captors, send her to France, or keep her in England—but they were all dangerous. Finally, Elizabeth decided to keep Mary in England under house arrest. The Scottish queen would spend the rest of her life under guard, shuttling from one royal place to another in northern England. She would never see her son or Scotland again.

Elizabeth had other worries besides her ever-scheming cousin. In December 1568, her attention again turned to international affairs. Protestants in the Netherlands were appealing for help in resisting an invasion by Spain. Queen Elizabeth responded to their plea and dispatched 7,000 English troops to the Netherlands. This war, eventually called the Eighty Years War, dragged on and used up much of the English treasury.

In England, religious conflicts were erupting once again. A Catholic rebellion in northern England had been brewing for months, stirred up by Mary. In November 1569, 300 armed Catholic citizens burst into a cathedral in the northern city of Durham.

*The Cathedral of Durham in northern England, where angry Catholic citizens destroyed the contents of the Protestant church*

They destroyed every Protestant symbol and burned English Bibles. Priests then held a Catholic mass in the Protestant church.

Elizabeth's troops quickly stopped the uprising, but its aftermath, known as the Northern Rebellion, was bloody. The common people suffered the most. Their crops were burned, and their farm animals became food for the army. Hundreds of people were killed; at least 800 perished on the gallows. Corpses littered northern England.

Elizabeth ended the Northern Rebellion, but she paid a price. She was excommunicated, or officially excluded, from the Roman Catholic Church. The pope declared that English Catholics were no longer obligated to honor or obey the queen. Elizabeth was declared a heretic and enemy of the true faith.

In return, Elizabeth increased the fines for not attending the Church of England. Later, it would be considered treason to convert to Roman Catholicism, and all Catholic priests would be forced to leave England. In the meantime, some people plotted to kill Queen Elizabeth.

*Sir Francis Walsingham (1532-1590)*

Elizabeth knew she couldn't trust anyone, especially Mary. So she set up an elaborate secret service organization, headed by Sir Francis Walsingham. As chief spy-master, Walsingham placed 70 agents in various European countries. They kept him informed of plots against the queen and up to date on the growing political and religious tensions in Europe. In 1571, Elizabeth's spies discovered an assassination plot. The conspirators were Mary; Roberto Ridolfi, an agent of the pope; and the Duke of Norfolk, a rich Catholic nobleman. Their scheme collapsed, however, when they failed to get Catholic support abroad. A year later, Elizabeth ordered Norfolk's execution.

All the while, Elizabeth was still considering possible husbands—not that she was going to marry any of them. Her foreign relations often grew stronger when leaders of other countries thought they might have a chance to become her husband. While they waited and wondered if they had won Elizabeth's heart, the crafty queen had the advantage, politically and personally.

In 1578, the 45-year-old queen courted the Frenchman Francis, Duke of Alençon. Elizabeth enjoyed the fun of flirtation with the short 24-year-old duke whose face was scarred by smallpox. But many people in England did not share the queen's enthusiasm for this man she called Frog.

A radical Protestant named John Stubbs published a pamphlet opposing the rumored marriage. His attack on the queen brought dire results. As the butcher's cleaver drove through his wrist, chopping off his right hand, Stubbs raised his hat with his left hand and cried, "God save Queen Elizabeth!" and then fainted. In September 1581, Elizabeth announced she no longer wanted to marry

Alençon. She had changed her mind. The Frenchman sailed home with Elizabeth's parting gift of 10,000 English pounds.

While Elizabeth was playing the courtship game, her former suitor, Robert Dudley, secretly got married. The queen's temper flared, and she sent Dudley to prison briefly for his deception.

Then Elizabeth had to deal with more serious problems. Once again, she was the target of an assassination plot. In January 1585, Walsingham suspected that Mary was scheming to kill Elizabeth. He moved Mary to a new location and secretly examined her personal belongings, looking for evidence. He found what he needed—a letter from Mary agreeing to a plot by Anthony Babington to kill Elizabeth.

Babington and his band of conspirators were swiftly arrested, tried, and executed. There was no escape for Mary. The evidence proved her guilt, and Parliament demanded Mary's head. Elizabeth hesitated. She had a habit of trying to avoid making decisions. But after months of wavering, Elizabeth finally signed her cousin's death warrant. On February 8, 1587, the ax fell, beheading Mary, the banished queen of Scotland.

After Mary's death, Elizabeth erupted into a temper tantrum. She had raged in anger before, once boxing her secretary of state's ears, another time throwing her slipper at Walsingham's face, and even

punching those who displeased her. This time, Elizabeth blamed everyone else for Mary's death. She denied having ordered the execution.

Her councilors had acted within the law, but they quaked in fear as the queen hurled terrible accusations at them. This dramatic exhibition of anger may have all been staged. Perhaps she hoped

*Mary, Queen of Scots, was beheaded on February 8, 1587, for plotting to kill Queen Elizabeth I.*

**67**

*William Cecil (1520-1598) was the chief adviser to Queen Elizabeth I for most of her reign.*

to escape the wrath of Catholics all over Europe for the death of Mary.

Elizabeth specifically directed her anger toward her closest adviser, William Cecil. He often had to ride out the storms of her anger. He wrote that all

servants "must sometimes bear the cross words, as I myself have had long experience." This time, the queen banished Cecil from her court.

Four days after Mary's death, Elizabeth wrote to James VI, denying she had ordered the execution of his mother.

> *I would you knew (though not felt) the extreme dolor [grief] that overwhelms my mind, for that miserable accident which (far contrary to my meaning) hath befallen ... I beseech you that as God and more know, how innocent I am ... I am not of so base a lineage, nor carry so vile a mind ... for your part, think you have not in the world a more loving kinswoman, nor a more dear friend than myself ... Elizab. R.*

Two months after Mary's execution, the uproar over her death began to subside.

Assassination plots decreased for some time. By April 1587, Cecil was back in Elizabeth's court, having weathered another one of her storms. Soon it was summer, the time Elizabeth always set aside to tour the countryside and see her subjects.

# 7 ENTERTAINING ROYALTY

The first stop on the queen's summer tour was Theobalds, William Cecil's country estate. Theobalds had once been a small house. But after 20 years of improvements for the queen's visits, it was now a magnificent mansion and one of Elizabeth's favorite places. It was a symbol of status with its ornate Tudor architecture.

For many years, Elizabeth had been taking long summer journeys, called progresses. She had been the guest of more than 400 of her wealthiest subjects over the years. Wherever she went, she created a glorious spectacle. When she had a chance, she talked with her beloved people of England. She listened to their concerns and often followed through with solutions. Sometimes she accepted a

*Hundreds of people traveled with Queen Elizabeth I on her summer processions throughout England.*

spur-of-the-moment invitation to go into a nearby house for refreshments. One person noted that Elizabeth was hailed:

> *with great acclamations and signs of joy as is customary in this country. ... She ordered her carriage to be taken sometimes where the crowd seemed thickest, and stood up and thanked the people.*

Her journeys took her on small country roads, but the royal entourage was a huge display. The queen traveled on horseback or in a litter. Hundreds of lords and ladies in exquisite attire and mounted on fine horses accompanied her. There was a multitude of servants and courtiers, all decked out in colorful clothes of crimson, blue, yellow, purple, and green.

Of course, the focus of attention was the queen in all her splendor. In Tudor times, magnificence equaled power and greatness. Elizabeth took great care to present herself as a majestic monarch on her progresses. She chose gowns of silk, velvet, satin, or taffeta, adorned with gems and pearls. Emblems of spiders and pansies decorated some of her dresses. Her ruffs were starched, and she wore the ever-widening farthingale to make her skirt expand as wide as possible.

Then she added her jewels. People often

wondered how she could carry the weight of so many diamonds and pearls. Among her magnificent gems were the long pearl ropes formerly owned by Mary, Queen of Scots. Elizabeth did not disappoint the crowds who flocked to see her along the way.

Transporting the queen's clothes, jewelry, documents, supplies, linens, utensils, equipment, and royal bed required at least 400 carts and 2,400 packhorses. Traveling about the country was very costly and put a drain on the royal treasury

A good meal was important in the Elizabethan court. Although poor people ate a humble diet of bread, fish, and cheese, the rich enjoyed a large variety of foods. They might serve beef, pork, lamb, rabbit, or even peacock and pigeons. Fruits and vegetables weren't considered as important as meats and tasty breads. Elizabeth's court served extravagant desserts such as cakes, tarts, pastries, and fruits with sugary syrups. Marzipan, a sweet pastry of ground almonds and sugar, was molded into shapes of animals, fruits, birds, and baskets. Sometimes a fine sugar mixture was modeled into bowls, glasses—or just about anything—and decorated elaborately.

However, in the queen's mind, these visits saved money for the royal court, because her hosts fed and housed them. No matter how much it cost the citizens of England, it was a great honor to host their queen and her court. Sometimes it produced rewards and political perks such as knighthoods.

The queen's hosts also enjoyed providing lavish entertainment for her. They competed to outdo each other. Attractions included pageants, banquets, plays, dances, fireworks, songs, and hunting trips. The most extravagant and costly entertainment, remembered as the best of all progresses, was at Kenilworth in 1575.

Robert Dudley, her host and old friend, rode out to meet Elizabeth and escort her to the castle. Approaching the gatehouse at 8 P.M., the queen focused her attention on the lake, where she saw a brilliant display:

*[A] floating island, bright blazing with torches, on which were clad in silks the Lady of the Lake and two nymphs waiting on her, who made a speech to the Queen of the antiquity and owners of the castle.*

The Lady explained that she had kept possession of the castle since King Arthur's days, but now she offered it to the queen. It is said that Elizabeth answered back that she thought it was already hers. In fact, she had given Kenilworth Castle to Dudley.

The following days brought music, dancing, hunting, masques, plays, a plentiful banquet, fireworks, and water pageants. Elizabeth attended a

*Kenilworth Castle in Warwickshire, England, where Queen Elizabeth I was lavishly entertained.*

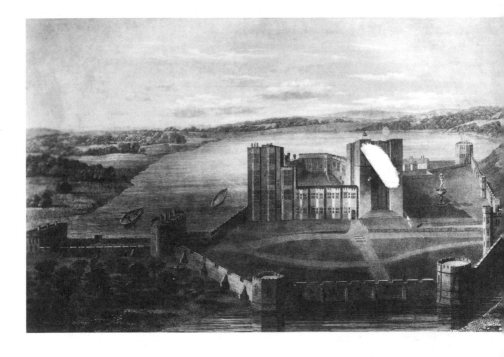

bearbaiting in the inner courtyard of the castle. The event featured 13 bears and several dogs, who tormented the bears. Elizabeth's stay at Kenilworth was a huge success. Her courtiers declared it a unique experience, and local people never forgot the queen's visit.

When Elizabeth returned to London, she shared the delights of her progress with her subjects. The details of her visit to Kenilworth were printed and distributed to the people, as was done for all her progresses. The popular pamphlets served to enhance her reputation as Good Queen Bess.

There were many festivities in London, as well. The royal court often moved from one palace to another. Wherever the court was, it was a lively place. Evenings were filled with pageants, masques, and performances of plays by William Shakespeare and Ben Jonson. Elizabeth enjoyed the theater and had her own theater group, the Queen's Men. Since music was important to Elizabeth, she kept a 30-member orchestra at her court. Music could fill the air whenever Elizabeth commanded.

To Elizabeth's delight, poets and playwrights often made her the subject of their writings. Works like Edmund Spenser's poem, "The Faerie Queene," celebrated her merits and virtues. She was portrayed as a goddess, a heroine from the Bible, or sometimes a lady of chivalry. Indeed, Elizabeth was

an interesting person and a lively queen. An English writer described her:

William Shakespeare entertained Queen Elizabeth I by reading his poetry and plays to her.

> The ordinary Englishmen saw in King Hal's full blooded daughter a queen after their own heart. She swore, she spat, she struck with her fist when she was angry; she roared with laughter when she was amused.

Most important to Elizabeth, though, was that she was loved and adored by her subjects. ✍

# 8 WAR WITH SPAIN

The Elizabethan Age—as these years of prosperity and lavish entertainment came to be called—was a glorious time for England. It was sometimes called the Golden Age, and the queen was proudly called Gloriana, a name given to her by poets and artists. But relationships with foreign countries, especially Spain, were strained.

By the late 1580s, Spain and England were on a political collision course. For years, Elizabeth's spies had watched Spain, looking for any signs that the country might be planning to invade England. In 1587, Elizabeth received word that King Philip II of Spain was preparing to attack her country with an armada of 130 warships and 30,000 men. He wanted to overthrow Elizabeth and take control of the

*The Spanish Armada made its way up the English Channel in 1587 to invade England.*

English throne. But Elizabeth decided to strike first, and fast. She unleashed the admiral of the English navy, Sir Francis Drake, on Spain.

Drake set out from Plymouth, England, with 24 ships and nearly 3,000 men. On April 19, 1587, he sailed into the harbor at Cadiz, Spain. Drake and his seamen looted and burned every Spanish ship in the harbor. As flames licked kegs of gunpowder, explosions pierced the air. Those onshore heard the

*The English navy caught the Spanish by surprise when they burned the Spanish Armada at Cadiz, Spain, in 1587.*

crackling and hissing of burning timber. Some said the flames made the city as bright as day.

The sneak attack by the English delayed Philip's military plans by more than a year. But it increased his determination to crush England and restore Catholicism to all of Europe. For 10 years, Elizabeth's privateers, her official royal pirates, had been raiding Spanish treasure ships. Elizabeth used the stolen treasure to help run her government and pay off debts incurred by previous reigns. In 1580, Drake, the queen's "deare pyrat," had returned from a voyage around the world with a fortune in gold, silver, and diamonds seized from the Spanish. These raids added to Philip's fury over the years.

> *Sir Francis Drake (1543?–1596) was an explorer, a sea captain, and a pirate. From 1577 to 1580, Drake sailed around the world, looting ships and trading in spices and slaves. His voyage made him the first Englishman to sail around the world, and he became England's hero. King Philip II of Spain demanded that Drake be punished for his deeds of piracy. But instead, Queen Elizabeth honored him by making him a knight.*

Now, a Spanish invasion that had worried Elizabeth for 30 years was becoming a reality. On July 19, 1588, the Spanish Armada was sighted off the English coast at Cornwall. It was said that Elizabeth's naval commanders, Drake and Lord Admiral Charles Howard, were at Plymouth Hoe playing a game of lawn bowls when the news came. With the enemy barely 50 miles (80 km) away, the story was told that Drake insisted there was time to finish his game.

The next morning, the English navy made its move, pulling its vessels out of Plymouth Harbor. With newer, smaller, and faster ships, the English navy managed to slip behind the Spanish Armada. The Spanish ships, heavy with horses and about 30,000 troops, moved at barely 2 miles (3.2 km) per hour. The English pursued the great Spanish fleet up the English Channel.

On July 27, 1588, the Armada anchored off the French port of Calais. At midnight on July 28, Howard sent eight ships to Calais, loaded with explosives. As they neared the Spanish fleet, the English set their ships on fire and escaped in rowboats. The blazing ships with no one onboard plowed through the curved row of Spanish ships.

The next day a fiery sea battle raged for nine hours. Unaware that the English had run out of ammunition, the crippled Spanish Armada retreated. Ferocious storms battered the ships on their journey around Ireland on their way back to Spain. Only 67 of Spain's 130 ships made it back.

More than 20,000 Spanish sailors lost their lives. The English lost no ships, and 100 men died in battle. However, English sailors had other problems.

Diseases like dysentery and typhus were killing more men than they were losing in battle.

Expecting a land invasion by Spain, Elizabeth rallied her troops at Tilbury on the Thames River to encourage them. Robert Dudley managed the lavish event. His plan included much pageantry and spectacle.

*Queen Elizabeth I gave an encouraging speech to her troops at Tilbury, Essex.*

The soldiers paraded before their queen. Mounted on a white horse, Elizabeth was dressed in white velvet adorned with silver armor. There, she made one of the great speeches of her life:

> *Let tyrants fear. I have so behaved myself, that under God I have placed my chiefest strength and safeguard in the loyal hearts and good will of my subjects. Wherefore I am come among you at this time, for my recreation and pleasure, being resolved in the midst and heat of the battle to live and die amongst you all, to lay down for my God, and for my kingdom and for my people mine honor and my blood run in the dust.*
>
> *I know I have the body but of a weak and feeble woman, but I have the heart and stomach of a king, and of a king of England. ...*

Spanish troops did not invade England's shore. The defeat of the Spanish Armada made Elizabeth famous. But her joy in the great victory was soon followed by grief. Suffering from exhaustion and stomach pains, Dudley died on his way home to Kenilworth. When Elizabeth heard this, she shut herself in her room and refused to speak. Finally, William Cecil ordered her door to be broken down.

Grief-stricken, Elizabeth put on a brave face to celebrate the victory over Spain. On November 26,

*Although Queen Elizabeth I lived in England all her life, she had political dealings with many European countries, shown here with modern boundaries.*

1588, she went to St. Paul's Cathedral to give public thanks for the great victory. There had not been such a glittering procession since her coronation.

The defeat of the Spanish Armada brought praise for Elizabeth at home and abroad. But her problems were not over. Future difficulties would overshadow her triumph.

# Chapter
# 9 END OF AN AGE

~~~✦~~~

Despite her declining years, Elizabeth still thought of herself as a young queen. She used lots of rouge and makeup to cover up her smallpox scars and aging skin. An auburn wig and magnificent youthful gowns became her trademarks. One observer noted that she was a woman "whom time had surprised." Elizabeth lamented that it was a curse to have a young mind in an old body.

The last two decades of Elizabeth's reign saw a new generation come of age and enter the royal court. These swashbuckling young men yearned for glory and adventure. A newcomer to the court was Robert Devereux, Earl of Essex, the dashing stepson of Robert Dudley. He soon became the queen's favorite and served as master of the horse. More than

*In her later years, Queen Elizabeth I tried to make herself look young with makeup, wigs, and beautiful clothes.*

30 years her junior, 22-year-old Essex was the lead-
ing flirt and wit at the royal court. Elizabeth enjoyed
his company and often allowed him to treat her with
playful disrespect.

The death of Elizabeth's spymaster Walsingham
brought another young courtier into the queen's
inner circle. In 1590, the clever, hardworking Robert
Cecil, son of William Cecil, became England's secretary of state.

Another person who gained the queen's favor
was Sir Walter Raleigh. This soldier, explorer, and
poet represented the bold, restless spirit of the new
young courtiers. Between 1584 and 1589, he organ-
ized five expeditions to the New
World and staked a claim for
England in North America.

Meanwhile, the con-
flict with Spain dragged
on. Raids and threats
on both sides occurred
without declaring war.
There was trouble,
too, within Elizabeth's
court. Essex, the
queen's favorite courtier,
led a revolt against her.
Elizabeth had him arrested
and tried for treason. He was

*Sir Walter
Raleigh (1552?-
1618) was an
English writer
and explorer.*

executed on February 25, 1601. The death of Essex was a personal tragedy for the queen.

The Elizabethan Age was coming to an end. The reign of Queen Elizabeth I had been a lavish spectacle, but now her court lacked money. Elizabeth resorted to selling her father's heirlooms and some of her royal lands to help pay for the country's military expenses. Trade had been badly damaged by the war with Spain, and the economy was suffering. Poor citizens roamed the countryside.

*Robert Devereux, Earl of Essex (1566-1601) was the last of Queen Elizabeth I's favorites in her court.*

Parliament enacted the Poor Laws, making the state responsible for the care of the needy. Then England took action to strengthen its economy. With the establishment of the British East India Company, England entered the arena of world trade, dominating it for the next three centuries.

England was gaining back some of its strength, but the queen was growing frail. At the opening of her last Parliament, she staggered on the steps to the throne under the weight of her heavy robes and crown. But she had not lost her political skill. On November 30, 1601, 68-year-old Elizabeth delivered what would later be known as her Golden Speech. She summarized her reign and reminded Parliament of her love for her people and her country:

*Queen Elizabeth I presiding over the English Parliament*

*I do assure you there is no prince that loveth his subjects better. ... I count the glory of my crown, that I have reigned with your loves.*

*To be a king and wear a crown is a thing more grievous to them that see it than it is to them that bear it. For myself, I was never so much enticed with the glorious name of a king or royal authority of a queen as delighted that God had made me His instrument to maintain His truth and glory and to defend this kingdom. ... You never have had nor shall have any [royal authority] that will be more careful and loving.*

*Elizabeth I was a woman of many talents and interests. She especially enjoyed riding horses and hunting. Often, she took long walks and had picnics in the forest. Not only did she enjoy the theater and musical entertainment, she also was a skilled musician. She played a virginal, a small keyboard instrument, and a lute, an instrument similar to a guitar. Elizabeth was quite a good dancer, she loved to sing, and she often wrote poetry.*

After her speech, Elizabeth invited every delegate to come forward and kiss her hand.

Elizabeth lived a quiet life for more than a year. She stayed to herself, often physically weak or emotionally dejected. She was deeply troubled that her dear Essex had turned against her, and it broke her heart to have him executed. She now felt extremely alone. She lost some of her fighting spirit and her wit. When a visitor read one of his rhymes to her, she remarked, "When thou dost feel creeping time at thy gate, these fooleries will please thee less; I am past my relish for such matters."

The queen was nearing the end of her reign. In September 1602, she turned 69, a very old age for the time. She had reigned as England's monarch for nearly 45 years and had outlived her friends as well as her enemies. Robert Cecil watched her decline physically and mentally, while he tried to make plans for the future of England.

There was still the question of who would take over the throne. Elizabeth had not named anyone to succeed her. Most of her councilors assumed she would choose James VI of Scotland. By this time, Elizabeth and James had put aside their differences and often advised each other on political matters. But Elizabeth had not officially named him as the next ruler of England.

By March 1603, Elizabeth isolated herself at Richmond Palace with a few of her attendants. Her days and nights were spent resting in a chair by the fire or standing in one place for hours on end. Encouraged by her attendants to rest, Elizabeth laid down on some cushions on the floor. For two days, she refused to move. Her doctor examined her, and her attendants tried to move her. When Cecil came to visit, he said she must go to bed. With a last spurt of her old spirit, she replied, "Little man, little man, the word must is not used to princes."

Elizabeth finally grew so weak, she could not resist when her attendants carried her to bed. She asked for music to be played, and this consoled her for a while. Cecil and the other councilors continued to ask her for a name—the person who would

*Painting of Elizabeth I's death by Paul Delaroche is displayed in the Louvre in Paris, France.*

*Elizabeth I is entombed at Westminster Abbey in London, England, next to her half-sister Mary (Bloody Mary).*

inherit her throne. But in her typical manner of putting off decisions, Elizabeth never spoke a name. In the early morning hours of March 24, 1603, Queen Elizabeth I of the House of Tudor died.

Immediately, Cecil wrote a proclamation, stating that the queen had died and that James VI of the House of Stuart would succeed her. The new king would bear the title King James I of England. Without delay, the royal councilors entered the Tower of London under the authority of the new king and prepared for his arrival. They also planned the funeral of Queen Elizabeth I, their honored monarch who had done so much for them.

Elizabeth's funeral was a huge spectacle, just like the England she had created. On April 28, 1603, thousands of mourners trekked to Westminster Abbey, where the queen would be entombed. Ahead of them was Elizabeth's coffin. On top was a life-sized carving of the queen adorned in her crown and royal robe. Seventeenth-century historian William Camden once predicted:

> *No oblivion shall ever bury the Glory of her Name for her happy and reknowned Memory still liveth, and shall for ever live in the Minds of men to all Posterity.*

The people would not forget their beloved Queen Elizabeth—Good Queen Bess, Gloriana—who had changed England forever. ℘

## ELIZABETH I'S LIFE

**1533**

Born at Greenwich
Palace, London,
England, September 7

**1536**

Mother Anne Boleyn
is executed

**1543**

Lives with stepmother
Katherine Parr;
tutored by William
Grindal and Roger
Ascham

**1535**

**1534**

Martin Luther
completes English
translation
of the Bible
into German

**1540**

Spanish explorer
Francisco Vásquez de
Coronado leads an
expedition into what is
now the southwestern
United States

## WORLD EVENTS

## 1553

Edward VI dies; sister Mary takes over the throne

## 1554

Imprisoned at Tower of London, then held under house arrest at Woodstock

## 1547

Father Henry VIII dies; brother Edward VI becomes king of England

## 1550

## 1545

The Catholic Counter-Reformation begins in Europe

## 1555

Artist Michelangelo completes his Pietà sculpture in Florence, Italy

## ELIZABETH I'S LIFE

### 1566

James VI of the House of Stuart is born (England's future King James I)

### 1558

Becomes queen of England on November 17

### 1559

Coronation ceremony on January 15; revives the Act of Supremacy

### 1562

Sends troops to France to help Protestants

## 1560

### 1558

Ferdinand I assumes title of Holy Roman Emperor

### 1564

Poet and playwright William Shakespeare is born

## WORLD EVENTS

**1569**

Excommunicated from the Roman Catholic Church

**1580**

Sir Francis Drake returns from trip around the world with fortunes for England

**1568**

Sends troops to the Netherlands to help Protestants, beginning the Eighty Years War

**1580**

**1571**

John Kepler, German astronomer, is born

**1580**

William Bourne makes the first published description of a submarine

## ELIZABETH I'S LIFE

### 1584

Sir Walter Raleigh
begins expeditions to
the New World to
stake claims
for England

### 1585

Babington Plot to
assassinate Elizabeth
is uncovered

### 1587

Orders Mary Queen of
Scots executed

**1585**

### 1586

William Camden
publishes his
*Britannia*, a guide
to the counties
of Britain

## WORLD EVENTS

**1601**

Delivers Golden
Speech to Parliament

**1603**

Dies March 24 at
Richmond Palace
in London; buried
at Westminster
Abbey in London

**1588**

English Navy defeats
the Spanish Armada
off the coast of France

**1600**

**1589**

Galileo Galilei
becomes professor
of mathematics at
University of Pisa

**1597**

The great English
scientist Francis
Bacon publishes
*Essays, Civil
and Moral*

**1603**

Heavy outbreak
of the plague
in England

**DATE OF BIRTH:** September 7, 1533

**BIRTHPLACE:** Greenwich Palace
London, England

**FATHER:** King Henry VIII
(1491–1547)

**MOTHER:** Anne Boleyn
(1500?–1536)

**EDUCATION:** Private tutors

**SPOUSE:** none

**CHILDREN:** none

**DATE OF DEATH:** March 24, 1603

**PLACE OF BURIAL:** Westminster Abbey
London, England

## IN THE LIBRARY

Ashby, Ruth. *Elizabethan England.* New York: Benchmark Books, 1999.

Drake, Jane, ed. *Queen Elizabeth I.* London: Jarrold Publishing, 1993.

Greenblatt, Miriam. *Elizabeth and Tudor England.* New York: Benchmark Books, 2002.

Thomas, Jane Resh. *Behind the Mask: The Life of Queen Elizabeth I.* New York: Clarion Books, 1998.

Newberry, Elizabeth. *Tower Power: Tales From the Tower of London.* Surrey, England: Historic Royal Palaces, 2004.

## LOOK FOR MORE SIGNATURE LIVES BOOKS ABOUT THIS ERA:

Christopher Columbus: *Explorer of the New World*

Nicolaus Copernicus: *Father of Modern Astronomy*

Galileo: *Astronomer and Physicist*

Johannes Gutenberg: *Inventor of the Printing Press*

Michelangelo: *Sculptor and Painter*

Francisco Pizarro: *Conqueror of the Incas*

William Shakespeare: *Playwright and Poet*

### ON THE WEB

For more information on *Elizabeth I*, use FactHound to track down Web sites related to this book.

1. Go to *www.facthound.com*
2. Type in a search word related to this book or this book ID: 0756509882
3. Click on the *Fetch It* button.

FactHound will find the best Web sites for you.

### HISTORIC SITES

Tower of London
London, England
To visit where Elizabeth was imprisoned

Westminster Abbey
London, England
To visit where Queen Elizabeth I is entombed

**armada**
large fleet of ships

**bearbaiting**
the practice of setting dogs upon a chained bear

**bowls**
a game in which players roll balls at an object

**cambric**
thin white linen or cotton fabric

**courtier**
an attendant at a royal court

**farthingale**
a hoop worn beneath a skirt to expand it

**heresy**
a belief that contradicts religious teaching

**inquest**
an official hearing in front of a jury

**jousting**
a form of combat in medieval times where two mounted knights charge at each other with spears

**litter**
a hand-carried couch with poles on each side, used to transport one person

**masques**
symbolic drama performed by masked actors

**menagerie**
a place where animals are kept and trained

**Privy Council**
officials chosen by a British monarch to give advice

**swashbuckling**
swaggering, daring, adventurous

## Chapter 1

Page 10, line 11: Wallace MacCaffrey. *Elizabeth I.* London: Edward Arnold, 1993, p. 18.

Page 10, line 16: Carole Levin, Jo Eldridge Carney, and Debra Barrett-Graves, eds. *Elizabeth I: Always Her Own Free Woman.* Burlington, Vt.: Ashgate, 2003, p. 222.

Page 10, line 19: Ibid., p. 222.

Page 14, line 3: John Foxe. *John Foxe's Book of Martyrs, Book 11* (1583 ed.) [Electronic version]. Humanities Research Institute. Sheffield, UK: University of Sheffield. http://hri.shef.ac.uk/foxe/single/book11/11_1583_1484.html

Page 15, line 13: Susan Watkins. *The Public and Private Worlds of Elizabeth I.* London: Thames and Hudson, 1998, p. 36.

## Chapter 2

Page 19, line 24: Carolly Erickson. *The First Elizabeth.* New York: Simon & Schuster, Inc., 1983, p. 20.

Page 20, line 9: Anne Somerset. *Elizabeth I.* New York: Alfred A. Knopf, 1999, p. 5.

Page 23, line 2: Elizabeth Jenkins. *Elizabeth the Great.* New York: Coward, McCann & Geoghegan, 1959, p. 14.

Page 25, line 11: *Elizabeth I* (Somerset). p. 11.

## Chapter 3

Page 35, line 6: "Mary I." Tudors and the Tower. http://tudors.crispen.org/tower/mary_i.html.

## Chapter 4

Page 39, line 10: *Elizabeth I* (Somerset). p. 57.

Page 40, line 5: *The First Elizabeth.* pp. 158–159.

Page 41, line 28: *The Public and Private Worlds of Elizabeth I.* p. 45.

Page 42, line 8: "Elizabeth I." http://englishhistory.net/tudor/monarchs/eliz2.html.

Page 43, line 4: *The First Elizabeth.* p. 163.

Page 46, line 10: "Elizabeth I." http://englishhistory.net/tudor/monarchs/eliz2.html.

## Chapter 5

Page 50, line 8: Leah S. Marcus, Janel Mueller, and Mary Beth Rose, eds. *Elizabeth I: Collected Works.* Chicago: The University of Chicago Press, 2000, p. 59.

Page 54, line 7: *The First Elizabeth.* p. 209.

## Chapter 6

Page 57, line 7: William Camden. *The History of the Most Renowned and Victorious Princess Elizabeth Late Queen of England.* Chicago: The University of Chicago Press, 1970, pp. 29–30.

Page 65, line 26: Alison Weir. *The Life of Elizabeth I.* New York: Ballantine Books, 2003, p. 61.

Page 69, line 1: Ibid., pp. 227–228.

Page 69, line 7: Jane Dunn. *Elizabeth and Mary: Cousins, Rivals, Queens.* New York: Alfred A. Knopf, 2004, p. 411.

## Chapter 7

Page 72, line 4: *Elizabeth I* (Somerset). pp. 372–373.

Page 75, line 1: *Life of Elizabeth I.* p. 299.

Page 77, line 3: David Loades. *Elizabeth I.* London: Hambledon and London, 2003, p. 319.

## Chapter 8

Page 84, line 5: Clark Hulse. *Elizabeth I: Ruler and Legend.* Urbana, Ill.: University of Illinois Press, 2003, p. 107.

## Chapter 9

Page 87, line 6: Lacey Baldwin Smith. *The Elizabethan World.* Boston: Houghton Mifflin Company, 1972, p. 258.

Page 91, line 1: Steven W. May, ed. *Queen Elizabeth I: Selected Works.* New York: Washington Square Press, 2004, pp. 86–87.

Page 92, line 1: Lytton Strachey. *Elizabeth and Essex: A Tragic History* [Electronic version]. New York: Harcourt Brace, 1928. http://www.athelstane.co.uk/strachey/elizessx/essex17.htm.

Page 92, line 28: "Queen Elizabeth I." http://englishhistory.net/tudor/monarchs/eliz5.html.

Page 95, line 18: *The Public and Private Worlds of Elizabeth I.* p. 197.

# Select Bibliography

Camden, William. *The History of the Most Renowned and Victorious Princess Elizabeth Late Queen of England.* Chicago: The University of Chicago Press, 1970.

Dobson, Michael, and Nicola J. Watson. *England's Elizabeth: An Afterlife in Fame and Fantasy.* Oxford: Oxford University Press, 2002.

Doran, Susan. *Queen Elizabeth I.* New York: New York University Press, 2003.

Dunn, Jane. *Elizabeth and Mary: Cousins, Rivals, Queens.* New York: Alfred A. Knopf, 2004.

Erickson, Carolly. *The First Elizabeth.* New York: Simon & Schuster, Inc., 1983.

Hulse, Clark. *Elizabeth I: Ruler and Legend.* Urbana, Ill.: University of Illinois Press, 2003.

Jenkins, Elizabeth. *Elizabeth the Great.* New York: Coward, McCann & Geoghegan, 1959.

Levin, Carole, Jo Eldridge Carney and Debra Barrett-Graves, eds. *Elizabeth I: Always Her Own Free Woman.* Burlington, Vt.: Ashgate, 2003.

Loades, David. *Elizabeth I.* London: Hambledon and London, 2003.

MacCaffrey, Wallace. *Elizabeth I.* London: Edward Arnold, 1993.

Marcus, Leah S., Janel Mueller, and Mary Beth Rose, eds. *Elizabeth I: Collected Works.* Chicago: University of Chicago Press, 2000.

May, Steven W., ed. *Queen Elizabeth I: Selected Works.* New York: Washington Square Press, 2004.

Picard, Liza. *Elizabeth's London: Everyday Life in Elizabethan London.* New York: St. Martin's Press, 2003.

Ridley, Jasper. *Elizabeth I: The Shrewdness of Virtue.* New York: Viking, 1987.

Ross, Josephine. *Suitors to the Queen: The Men in the Life of Elizabeth I of England.* New York: Coward, McCann & Geoghegan, Inc., 1975.

Smith, Lacey Baldwin. *The Elizabethan World.* Boston: Houghton Mifflin Company, 1972.

Somerset, Anne. *Elizabeth I.* New York: Alfred A. Knopf, 1999.

Starkey, David. *Elizabeth: The Struggle for the Throne.* New York: HarperCollins Publishers, Inc., 2001.

Watkins, Susan. *The Public and Private Worlds of Elizabeth I.* London: Thames and Hudson, 1998.

Weir, Alison. *The Life of Elizabeth I.* New York: Ballantine Books, 2003.

Act of Supremacy, 46
Act of Uniformity, 46
Alençon, Francis Duke of, 65–66
Anne of Cleves (stepmother), 27
Ascham, Roger, 28
Ashridge House, 25

Babington, Anthony, 66
bearbaiting, 76
Bell Tower, 11, 36
Bible, 32
Black Death, 58
Bloody Mary. See Mary (sister)
Bloody Tower, 11
Boleyn, Anne (mother), 11, 12, 19,
    21–22, 23, 34
*Book of Common Prayer, The,* 46
Bothwell, Earl of, 59–62
British East India Company, 89
Bryan, Lady Margaret, 21, 22, 23
bubonic plague, 58
bynames, 20

Calais, France, 82
Camden, William, 95
Catharine of Aragon, 18, 19, 23
Catholics, 13–14, 18, 32, 33–34, 49,
    54–55, 59, 62–65
Cecil, Robert, 88, 92, 93, 95
Cecil, William, 41, 52, 68–69, 71, 88
Champernowne, Katherine "Kat," 25,
    30, 41
Charles (archduke of Austria), 51
Charles IX (king of France), 51
Chelsea Palace, 30
christenings, 19, 20
Church of England, 13–14, 18, 28, 42,
    62–65
Cranmer, Thomas, 14
Cromwell, Thomas, 23

Darnley, Lord Henry, 55, 58–59
desserts, 74
Devereux, Robert, 87–89, 91
diet, 74

diseases, 24, 46, 52–53, 58, 83
divorce, 18, 19
Drake, Sir Francis, 80, 81–82
drought, 40
Dudley, Amy, 52
Dudley, Robert, 41, 51–52, 54, 55, 66,
    74, 75, 83–84

education, 28–29, 31
Edward VI (brother), 24, 28, 30, 31–32,
    46
Eighty Years War, 62
Elizabethan Age, 15, 79
Elizabeth I
    appearance of, 44, 72, 87
    birth of, 19, 20
    bravery of, 10
    childhood of, 20–25, 27, 28
    christening of, 19
    coronation of, 42–46
    death of, 94
    education of, 28–29, 31
    excommunication of, 64
    fear of execution, 12
    funeral of, 95
    as godmother, 59
    illnesses of, 46, 52–53
    love of people for, 33, 41–42,
        43–46, 72, 77
    marriage and, 27–28, 40, 49–51,
        54, 57, 65–66
    money problems of, 62, 89, 91
    motto of, 41
    nicknames for, 15, 51, 79, 95
    as old woman, 87, 89–92
    plots against, 64–65, 66, 69
    reaction to ascension, 39
    during reign of Edward, 30
    during reign of Mary, 9–12,
        14–15, 32–36
    religion of, 28, 33–34
    royal council of, 41
    talents and interests of, 76, 91
    temper of, 66–69, 77
Elsynge Place, 25

Enfield Palace, 25, 30
England, conditions in, 36, 39–40
entertainment, 74–76, 91
Eric (prince of Sweden), 51
Essex, Earl of, 87–89, 91
executions, 12, 14, 22, 23, 29, 30, 32, 34, 37, 65, 66, 69, 89, 91
exploration, 88

"Faerie Queene, The" (Edmund Spenser), 76
famine, 37
Ferdinand (archduke of Austria), 51
food, 74
France, 58
Francis, Duke of Alençon, 65–66
Frederick (prince of Denmark), 51
Friar's Chapel at Greenwich, 19

Gloriana. See Elizabeth I
Golden Age of England, 15, 79
Golden Speech, 90–91
Good Queen Bess. See Elizabeth I
government, 40, 46, 51, 54, 89
Greenwich Palace, 19, 20, 22
Grey, Lady Jane, 32, 34
Grindal, William, 28, 30

Hatfield House, 21, 24, 25, 30, 32, 34, 36
Henry, Lord Darnley, 55, 58–59
Henry de Valois (duke of Anjou), 51
Henry Tudor. See Henry VIII (father)
Henry VIII (father), 13, 17–21, 22–24, 27, 29, 46
Hepburn, James, 59–62
heresy, 14, 37
House of Commons, 46
House of Lords, 46
House of Stuart, 20, 55, 59
House of Tudor, 17, 20, 32–33, 54
Howard, Catherine (stepmother), 27, 34
Howard, Charles, 81–82
Hundson, 22

illnesses, 24, 46, 52–53, 58, 83
invasion, 79, 81–82

James I (king of England). See James VI (king of Scotland)
James VI (king of Scotland), 59, 61, 92, 95
Jonson, Ben, 76

Kenilworth Castle, 74–76

Leicester, Earl of, 52. See also Dudley, Robert
literature, 76–77, 91
London, 40
Lord Protector, 54
Luther, Martin, 32

male heir to throne, 17–19, 22, 49
Mary, Queen of Scots, 40, 54–55, 58–62, 64, 65, 66–69, 69
Mary (sister), 9, 12–14, 18, 19, 20, 21, 22, 24, 32–34, 36–37, 39, 40
music, 76, 91, 93

names, 20
Netherlands, 62
Ninety-Five Theses (Martin Luther), 32
Norfolk, Duke of, 65
North America, 88
Northern Rebellion, 63–64

Parliament, 46, 50–51, 54, 89
Parr, Katherine (stepmother), 28, 29, 30
Philip II (king of Spain), 36–37, 50, 51, 79, 81
piracy, 81
poetry, 76, 91
Poor Laws, 89
poverty, 37, 40, 89
prison life, 10, 11–12, 34–36
progresses, 71–76
Protestants, 13–14, 18, 28, 32, 34–35, 37, 42, 49, 54–55, 62–65

Queen's Men, 76

Raleigh, Sir Walter, 88
rebellions, 63–64
Reformation, 32
religious conflicts, 12–14, 32, 33–34,
    36–37, 42, 46–47, 49, 54–55,
    62–65, 81
Riccio, Henry, 58–59
Richmond Palace, 92
Ridolfi, Roberto, 65
Rogers, John, 14
Roman Catholic Church, 13–14, 18, 32,
    34–35, 59, 62–65, 81
royal succession, 17–19, 22, 37, 49,
    52–55, 92–95

secret service organization, 64
Seymour, Edward, 30
Seymour, Jane (stepmother), 24
Seymour, Thomas, 30
Shakespeare, William, 76
smallpox, 52–53, 87
Spain, 37, 62, 79–82, 85, 88
Spanish Armada, 81–82, 85
Spenser, Edmund, 76
spies, 64
Stubbs, John, 65

theater, 76, 91
Theobalds estate, 71
Tower Green, 22
Tower of London, 9–12, 22, 34–36,
    42, 43
trade, 89
Traitor's Gate, 10, 35
treason, 9, 10, 30, 34, 64, 66

Virgin Queen. See Elizabeth I

Walsingham, Sir Francis, 64, 66, 88
Westminster Abbey, 44–45
Westminster Hall, 44, 46
Whitehall Palace, 42
White Tower, 11
Woodstock lodge, 12, 14–15, 36
Wyatt, Sir Thomas, 9, 34

Myra Weatherly writes for children and young adults from her home in South Carolina. Her interest in England and English literature began in childhood. Her undergraduate degree is in English, and she has traveled extensively in Great Britain.

## Image Credits